The
Perfect Cold
Warrior

To Joe Lowe
with best wishes

[signature]

Also by Gary Geddes

Poetry

POEMS, 1971
RIVERS INLET, 1972
SNAKEROOT, 1973
LETTER OF THE MASTER OF HORSE, 1973
WAR & OTHER MEASURES, 1976
THE ACID TEST, 1980
THE TERRACOTTA ARMY, 1984
CHANGES OF STATE, 1986
HONG KONG, 1987
SELECTED WRITINGS OF GARY GEDDES,
  (translated into Chinese by Peng Jia-lin), 1988
NO EASY EXIT /SALIDA DIFÍCIL, 1989
LIGHT OF BURNING TOWERS: POEMS NEW & SELECTED, 1990
GIRL BY THE WATER, 1994

Fiction

THE UNSETTLING OF THE WEST, 1986

Non-Fiction

LETTERS FROM MANAGUA: MEDITATIONS ON POLITICS AND ART, 1990

Drama

LES MAUDITS ANGLAIS, 1984

Translation

I DIDN'T NOTICE THE MOUNTAIN GROWING DARK, Poems of Li Pai and
  Tu Fu, with the assistance of George Liang, 1986

Criticism

CONRAD'S LATER NOVELS, 1980

Anthologies

20TH-CENTURY POETRY & POETICS, 1969, 1973, 1985, 1995
15 CANADIAN POETS TIMES 2, 1971, 1977, 1988
SKOOKUM WAWA: WRITINGS OF THE CANADIAN NORTHWEST, 1975
DIVIDED WE STAND, 1977
THE INNER EAR, 1983
CHINADA: MEMOIRS OF THE GANG OF SEVEN, 1983
VANCOUVER: SOUL OF A CITY, 1986
COMPAÑEROS: AN ANTHOLOGY OF WRITINGS ABOUT LATIN AMERICA,
  (co-edited with Hugh Hazelton), 1990
THE ART OF SHORT FICTION: AN INTERNATIONAL ANTHOLOGY, 1993

The Perfect Cold Warrior

BY

Gary Geddes

QUARRY PRESS

Some of these poems have appeared in *Quarry, The Observer, The Ottawa Citizen, The Observer Arvon Poetry Collection 1993, Nimrod: International Journal of Poetry & Prose, Take This Waltz: A Celebration of Leonard Cohen,* and *Index.* The author would like to thank the Ontario Arts Council, The Canada Council, Heritage Cultures and Languages, Multiculturalism Branch, Secretary of State, Bureau of International Cultural Relations at External Affairs, and Concordia University for moral and financial support. Individual thanks go to Hugh Hazelton, Emile Martel, John Asfour, Douglas Isaac, Mark Abley, Colin Browne, Izzat al- Ghazzawi, Ron Smith, and my wife Jan Geddes.

For assistance in the Middle East, I wish to thank Nawal Halawa, Subhe Qahawish, Maxine Kaufman Nunn of the Alternate Information Centre, The Canadian Embassy, Arab Studies Society, Palestinian Human Rights Information Centre, Albert Aghazarian, Bir Zeit University, An-Najah University,Bethlehem University, Hanan Awad of Palestinian P.E.N., Richard Sherwin at Bar Ilan University, Sarah Gilead and Bill Freedman at Haifa University, Mark Taylor of the Canadian Palestinian Studies Association and United Nations Works and Relief Agency, and my friends at the Jerusalem Hotel.

The publisher acknowledges the support of The Canada Council, the Ontario Arts Council, the Department of Canadian Heritage, and the Ontario Publishing Centre.

Canadian Cataloguing in Publication Data

Geddes, Gary, 1940 —
    The perfect cold warrior
Poems.
ISBN 1-55082-140-7

    I. Title.

PS8563.E3P47 1995   C811' .54   C95–900160-3
PR199.3.G4P47   1995

Cover art entitled "Four Boys" 1986, by Dennis Geden, Canadian, b. 1944, reproduced by permission of the artist.

Printed and bound in Canada by Tri-Graphic, Ottawa, Ontario.

CONTENTS

Alas I did not say what I should have. . . .
And form itself as always is betrayal.
— Czeslaw Milosz

The advantage of poetry over life is that poetry, if it is
sharp enough, may last. We are unnerved, I suppose, by
the thought that authenticity, in the poem, is not
produced by sincerity. We incline, in our anxiety for
formulas, to be literal: we scan Frost's face compulsively
for hidden kindness, having found the poems to be, by all
reports, so much better than the man. This assumes our
poems are our fingerprints, which they are not. And the
processes by which experience is changed — heightened,
distilled, made memorable — have nothing to do with
sincerity. The truth, on the page, need not have been
lived. It is, instead, all that can be envisioned.
— Louise Glück

1 The Drive

Doesn't every narrative lead back to Oedipus? Isn't storytelling always a way of searching for one's origins, speaking one's conflicts with the Law, entering into the dialectic of tenderness and hatred?

— Roland Barthes

Etymology

Sometimes during spelling-bee
I get to wondering about the origins
of words. *Parenthetical,* for example,

what does it have to do with parents?
This leads to questions
about my own murky origins

and images of my father in rut.
I consider the women in his life: my mother
long since dead from reproductive

cancer, 'that Bruner woman' who lives
near the construction site in Salcoats
and was built into family legend

while my step-mother gave birth to her
first and only natural child.
Others? Most likely, given the way

his rude, inquisitive hands
violate the space of guests, female
relatives, as if the body

and its parts are public property.
A Puritan when it comes to the sexual habits
of others, he can't bear to hear

a dirty joke spoken in mixed company,
complains of skimpy costumes, and even
near the end at eighty suspects himself

duped and cuckholded. I observe him,
aghast, the man who made me,
genetic coding and all, bequeathed

his weak back and poorly evolved
arthritic feet, his fishy inheritance
and love of boats, all those ancestors

scuttling among rocks and Scottish
estuaries. But that's not why I classify
each gesture, cross-examine witnesses

who claim to know him. It's the other
I seek, the one whose hands
stray from gillnet and carpentry,

healing labour, the time-
bomb of the father I carry like a
ticking clock inside.

Privilege

Ann's Grocery sits on the northwest corner
of Fourth and Commercial. A cross-walk
links her establishment with the brown-brick
of the Highland Apartments and our cheap

digs above the woodworking shop next door
at 1926. I dislike fetching groceries on the tab,
but Ann Motiuk doesn't seem to mind. She smiles
and asks about my step-mother before ringing up items

and entering the total in her book. It isn't the same
with the old man, who works sporadically for the railway
and only likes customers who pay cash, which he pockets
for his own purposes. I often loiter among the cereals

and Royal City canned goods on the off-chance
he'll disappear through the curtain for a leak or smoke.
The labels are dark blue with gold lettering
and conjure privilege. Once we had their peaches

for Sunday supper, after scalloped potatoes
and slices of fried bologna. The six peach halves
had been canned early, their edges firm
and resistant to the tongue's pressure. Ann is

at the counter when I make a beeline for the freezer.
Her son John is with me, a kid who works long hours
in the store and takes a lot of shit at school,
being called a *Bohunk* by the same brats whose parents

enjoy Ann's credit. Injustice will make a lawyer
of John. In the meantime, he develops a complex smirk
from biting off his anger with a smile. In a dressing-
gown the deep blue of Royal City labels, Queen

Ann surveys her domain. Shelves need stock, coolers
must be defrosted, and yesterday's white loaves
marked down. Flourescent lights hum and the cop
on the beat, stationed at the school crosswalk, talks

to a second batch of kids. Ann basks in the security
his presence offers, after a childhood of racists
and bullies in Winnipeg. "Hey, it's 8:30." She leans
against the cash register. "You two should be in class.

You in trouble or something? Expelled?" I place
the orange popsicle on the counter and fish in my pants
for the nickel earned washing the dog and vacuuming
the bleak corridor leading to our apartment. I shake

my head, drop the coin in Ann's outstretched hand, and
look up into her eyes, self-important, sole custodian
of classified information. John, court jester, is smirking
from the stool beside his mother. I pop the two sticks

in my mouth and blow into the wrapper. It balloons
around the frozen but not-yet-surgically-separated
twins prostrate inside. "The King is dead," I grin,
handing John his portion, "and school's been cancelled."

June, 1952. Sun spills shamelessly on my freckled arms,
on my schoolbag with its squashed peanut-butter sandwich;
the interurban growls along its fixed track to Cedar Cottage
and New Westminster. One spent nickel face-down on the glass.

The Rent

Days when the pay cheque
doesn't make it home
and my father rolls in late
from Lil the bootlegger's

reeking of stale beer, I know
a trip is in the works for me
to the landlord's place

at 49th and Fraser. I hate
having to offer excuses
for paying only a fraction
of the $40 rent. Mr. Gill,

as usual, is behind the counter
in his clothing store,
tallying invoices or pricing pairs

of socks and underwear.
My hands patrol my pockets
fingering trolley transfers
I've rolled, out of nervousness,

into little cylinders the shape
of cigarettes. If the envelope
contains $10 and no note

from my step-mother, I relay
her apologies and promise
to bring installments every week
until the debt is paid. He

always smiles and thanks me
for the cash; I don't recall
a single complaint or raised

eyebrow, but I hang around outside
until the shop is empty,
just in case. At 49th the city
slopes south to Marpole

and the sawmills of the Fraser
River. If you get a roll on,
you can coast over that sea

of sun-washed wood-chips
as far as Bellingham or Seattle,
where things might be different.
Among the stripped mirror-frames

and oiled blanket-boxes of friends,
I still associate the smell of cedar
with the affluence of others.

False Creek

My father keeps his gillnetter moored
over the winter at False Creek,
where a single mill remains and a few

local industries and trucking companies
occupy the shoreline and flat-land
under the Granville Bridge. I ride my bike
down Terminal Avenue, past railyards

and shipping-sheds, and leave it lying
on the wharf while I pump dry
the reeking bilge. The flats have their own

bouquet, especially at low-tide, a nauseating
funk of primal ooze that spawns
species predestined
to replace us. Everything in the boat

is damp and sometimes the water-level
rises over the floorboards in the cockpit,
where tin cans and other items float

and knock against the drum and ribs
as I bail furiously. My recurring
nightmare is to find the boat submerged,
only the mast protruding

from the black, oily water, pointing
its accusing finger at me. Minnows
and bottom-feeders will swim

through the cabin, brushing the glass
of the wheelhouse with cold gill
and gossamer fin. The compass
gives no direction; the eight spokes

of the helm a child's sun, passing
a night of wet, cold comfort
under the sea, in league with star-fish

and other creatures of the deep. I try
to escape this dream on my bicycle
but water impedes my movements,
the pedals turning in slow motion

and my heart pumping wildly
past the stalled cars and ghostly red traffic
light at Terminal and Main.

Trick or Treat

When I look at the bones of both feet
in the shoe store's x-ray machine
I can see they're crowded
by my new penny-loafers. My step-
mother jokes about skeletons

and Halloween costumes, though
she knows I'm dressing up
as a pirate. There were moments
I considered drag, having
established a routine at home

that is popular, sashaying
from a storage closet, awkwardly located
behind the oil heater. Cosmetics,
high heels, one of my step-mother's
discarded dresses. This is as close to sex

as I can venture, masquerading
as a woman, with apples or softballs
for breasts, depending on the effect
required. My father sometimes laughs,
embarrassed, then slaps my bum

and calls me a tart. I assume, incorrectly,
he means it as a compliment.
I love off-colour jokes, even if I don't
get the meaning. The flush they bring
to faces is better than rouge.

One elaborate joke my step-mother
told me employs the phrase
cooking the goose as a euphemism
for intercourse. The punch-line comes
when the woman declares herself

satisfied: *I guess the goose*
is cooked, the gravy's running
down my leg. At age eight
sex is a greater mystery
than x-rays. At eleven I pretend

to be fully informed about birds
and bees to escape a humiliating
explanation. On my last celebration
of All Soul's Eve, swashbuckling
from door to door for candies

and other hand-outs, an old man
stands between Dennis and me
and the half-closed door. *Hey, kids,*
hear about the lady who married
an x-ray technician? The man

wears a frayed dressing-gown
and felt slippers; there is grease
on his stubbled chin. I look down
at my new shoes and wish
I'd worn gumboots. The two coins

peer back at me through their leather lids
mumbling penny for your thought,
penny for the guy. The man clears phelgm
from his throat and grins: *Nobody*
could figure out what he saw in her.

Manitoba Hardware

I fondle buckets of bright nails in graduated
sizes, each with a metal garden claw
for raking into stiff brown bags. Flux,
taps, other plumbing fixtures,
pipes, and gleaming crescent wrenches
mounted on hooks according to size

like kids in photographs. Blinds, uncut glass,
packages of putty, padlocks,
hinges. Alladin's cave has nothing
more exciting than this to offer until the day
the first boxed television sets arrive
and the beauty of the tools fades

in the incandescent glow of talking heads.
Proof is here, in black and white,
for any fool to see: technology
restoring magic to our lives.
And there's our own Doug Hepburn,
the world's strongest man

eating eighty raw eggs, then lifting
a car and a platform with twenty-seven people
on the Ed Sullivan Show for millions to see,
my eyes pulled from set to lighted set
until he has eaten eight times eighty raw eggs
and the multiples of his greased, protruding muscles

glow silver as the second-hand Cadillac
he parks outside his gym on The Drive
near Venables. Tonight I'll bench-press
the coal bucket, containing Trixie
my neurotic spaniel, until the coffee table
groans and collapses under our combined

weight. Meanwhile, down the street,
dust from eight posses pursues the dust
of eight desperados into as many blind canyons
and a host of fading, inanimate objects
hang on in display cases and dark corners
oblivious to the new order.

Jewel in the Crown

I go to work for Mitch at age twelve,
picking up parts for his watch repairs
from wholesalers downtown, crystals,

hair-springs, balance wheels. As I ride
on the streetcar past Victory Square,
I can see the words NOT A SPROTT

scribbled as graffiti at street-level
on *The Sun* building. My sexual education
has just begun and I assume a sprott

is something girls possess that I haven't
yet seen. Only years later do I realize
it's the name of a city councillor

who is not the favourite of all her
constitutents. Mitch trusts me
to dress his windows freshly each week

with coloured paper and crepe that bleaches
in the afternoon sun, shifting the limited
stock of watches and jewelry into ever-new

positions. He's a marvel to me,
a polio victim at age sixteen, who wears time
in a lump on his back and can take

your measure at a glance, just as he'll diagnose
the problems in a wristwatch. He resembles
Peter Lorre with his hyper-thyroid eyes

and looks quite scary hunched over his bench
with the black plastic jeweller's glass
stuck in the folds of his right eye and held there

by bunching the muscles on the right side
of his face. I work for two dollars a week
every night after school, but sometimes

make an extra two bucks baby-sitting his kids
on the weekend. Mostly they sleep and I can
amuse myself by masturbating undetected

in the kitchen with the help of *Eaton's Catalogue*
and various skin-creams that line the glass
shelf of the bathroom. I never learn

how to mend time, but a long slow apprenticeship
in shame when his oldest daughter describes
how I have touched her with my penis.

My step-mother appears gently reproachful,
my father mutters about castration
from his oasis at the Canadian Legion, and

I never see the inside of Mitch's store
again. Years later newspaper
disclosures and trials throughout the country

will bring this memory home to me with a crash —
trust broken, indelible stamp, and a hump
to bear like an albatross upon my back.

Faust on Two Wheels, Going Like Hell

I cut a deal with my step-mother
to split the cost of a second-hand bike
for my thirteenth birthday. John

Pennington is graduating to a five-speed
for his deliveries at the drugstore,
so she agrees to contribute three dollars.

I hold that bike in awe because it's
John's and allows me to share his powers,
if only in my mind. He is sixteen,

worldly, and can make Diane Beskau
blush, when she never notices me
hang-dogging around her front porch.

He sings popular songs, including
one whose lyrics I deliciously misconstrue
about a drifter or no-good who feels blue

because his lover's *tits* are on the wall.
I am no surrealist and haven't heard of Picasso,
so I wait a long time to figure out

the logistics of that piece. Enunciation,
to my great joy, is not John's forte
and it takes me three decades to discover

the source of the lover's torment is not
an unresponsive mate who's turned away in bed,
but a *picture* on the wall, a wanted poster

of the departed. I worship that bike,
rubbed and annointed until there's a coat
of gold fleck paint on the rims a sixteenth

of an inch thick. This is my ticket
to paradise, my personal key to the city.
I cycle over Lion's Gate Bridge

pushing the old clunker up the grade
until I can watch foreign ships
ease their way into the Inner Harbour,

then spy on lovers at the beach
letting the sun and hot sand roast my weiner
while I dip French fries in ketchup

and try to appear inconspicuous.
Meanwhile, the bike grows more flambouyant,
sprouting bright plastic streamers

from the handlebars, metal rattlers
mounted to the frame with clothes-pins
to strike rotating spokes and shatter

the early morning silence of The Drive.
Reflector, head-light, rear-view mirror,
nothing is too good for my glamorous bike

until the September, two years later, when
I enter high school and the gold rims
underneath the porch turn brown.

The Other Cheek

When your knife slices through my jacket
into muscle and fatty tissue,
stopping so close to the stomach

wall the doctor in Emergency
keeps going on about good luck,
I refuse to press charges.

It wouldn't be sporting, your
mother in tears on the front-porch
saying you'll go to jail for sure

this time, after the stolen cars,
the break-ins. I finger the scar
just to the right of my navel, a worm

of elevated tissue about an inch long.
An inchworm. Consider the options:
more stones thrown at my back

along the route from school, agents
of revenge. Concepts are not your cup
of tea, though you chugalug *want, get,* and *take*

with the best of them. I have to decide fast,
my father's cab idling at the curb, my step-mother
with her purse and stained, pink uniform

and all those tables still to wait on
at Toot's Cafe. It happened at the bus-stop
on my way to church, though I felt nothing

and only noticed my shirt wet with blood
during hymn-sing. Charity, be damned.
Christ, in His mercy, is my guide.

I can't lose. Arch enemy in my debt
at last, less likely to cast stones
at my head than run interference.

I set aside revenge and choose forgiveness,
a stable investment that offers
power, insurance, safer than Lloyds.

Horatio at The Cut

When she bent to pick up the paper
and her dressing-gown fell open, I thought
the heavens had opened for me too. Go ahead,

call me Flynn. Willy, gimme another thirty
over here. No, the folded ones. You owe me
for yesterday. Fuck the time. Where was I?

So, Jesus, I says, did she think I had all day
to pat her pussy? A kid's got to make a living
too. Ask Frost about the paper-route not taken.

Frost? It's not that cold, she says. Besides,
it's plenty warm inside. Christ, the weight
hanging on that preposition made me hard.

But what's the point wasting my breath
on you stupid virgins. Jurgens Lotion Boys.
Jurgen off, that is. District supervisor's

my next move. Then I'll have plenty of time
to dally on collections. I'll pick up a case
at Lil's and give the ladies something more

than news. What's with the hockey shirt
in summer, dink? No one told you the Smucks
need ice? C'mere, I'll show you a thing or two

about stick-handling. Say, Charlie, when you make
the drop at Rexall's, pick up up a dozen safes
for me, eh? Strong ones. Might come in handy

tonight. When the Great Northern Special
rolls through, we'll see if we can place
a water-ball down the stack or wash the smile

off that asshole cop who rides the caboose
from Grandview Highway to the Terminal.
Now cut this shit and sell *The Province.*

Making It

Yes, there are coal sacks, the black
grainy kind made of rough hemp
that cause fingers and forearms to itch,
bottles to gather, pennies to earn

reselling lost or discarded items, beach-
combing sidewalks, concrete estuaries.
A brief career could be constructed
from such inauspicious beginnings,

collecting forgotten verses for janitors
and housewives, texts that lie
unnoticed in magazines or slim volumes,
grown dust-covered in libraries,

used-book stores. In the end, though,
I prefer to leave the stray bottles
where they wash up along roadsides,
sunlight reflected in the green

or brown glass, and pointing towards
some departed one whose destiny
has spun-out with a wave or kiss. Not even
inflating the price can convince me

to interfere with the shining hubcap
half-buried in gravel and dented
like Achilles' shield from fierce
combat. I leave my own choice detritus

in out-of-the-way places, collectibles
of no particular value, but able
to catch the eye, encourage speculation,
incite seduction in the ear.

Damaged Goods

My father brings home merchandise
from the warehouse at Macintosh Cartage
that's smoke-damaged, parts

of a shipment of plaster wall-hangings,
trios of air-borne ducks that can fly
in any direction or formation,
depending which way and on which wall

you hang them. Black velvet paintings,
exotic feminine profiles, chocolates,
and imported tea-sets. A trailor-load

of goodies up for grabs, already written-off
by the insurance company. Everyone
he knows in Grandview is on the alert,
making space for plaster drakes

and mallards, high-flyers all. There are
even dress-shirts that did not escape
unscathed inside their plastic packaging.

How he loves it, my skid-road Rockefeller,
Santa of the smoke-house, not just delivering
the goods, but dispensing largesse, his heart
expanding to the task. Even now the paternal

corpse speaks out, scripting my narrative.
Where is this man I seek to credit
and to blame? He is here inside, alien

but perfectly at home in his self-created
host. Big-time spender, eating my heart out,
distributing my organs among friends, a great squid
squirting his black ink through my veins,

authoring destiny, continuance,
the ball-and-chain of my being. No exile,
no extradition order, can touch him;

he has survived war, prohibition, the myth
of origins. Each day I kill and resurrect him
as required. Thesis, antithesis, dialectic
of desire, denying inheritance, yet

potlaching its resources. Father and son,
and that third duck in the plaster Trinity —
joker, trickster, monkey-king, wild card!

B.C. Collateral

Father takes the gold tooth I found
in the abandoned hospital in Rivers Inlet
and sells it for seven dollars at a pawn shop
on Hastings Street. Does the money feed us

or his habits; does it matter? He, too,
has a son's inheritance, bared roots
screaming for familiar soil. A century
of clearances strips the Highlands,

is no less brutal to the home order.
What does it seek to hide, the family
portrait? Straight backs, austere faces, flesh
dissolved behind masks, pocketed hands

evolving into clubs. The brutish empire
eats its sons, its daughters. For all his failures
I idolize him, construct legends
to barter with at school among those

whose fathers have only money or success:
the war, the deep-sea legacy,
a host of pocket-knives I promptly lost,
twelve schools in twelve years, a second chance

at family life after my mother died.
Gold teeth extracted in the antechambers
of Belsen serve as talismans
for those who blame their fathers

for the social order. I ponder that fierce-
rooted molar as if it were Yorick's
skull. No refuge for me
among the innocent. With luck

and a measure of forgiveness
I scribble poems instead of wreaking havoc.

Active Trading

I come by my taste for disaster
naturally, raised in a district
bounded by Commercial Drive,
Broadway, and Terminal Avenue:

money, showbiz, death, the secular
trinity. Weekends and after school,
I watch wrecks jockeyed
around the sheet-metal enclosure

at Clark and Hastings, the automobile
graveyard with its crushed Fords
and devastated Chevies occupying
common ground. Huge cranes,

meticulous, hoist an Edsel, casualty
of a species already endangered
on the drawing-board, to the privacy
of restoration shed, and a quaint

torpedo-nosed Studebaker, totalled
in a spectacular four-vehicle accident
on the TransCanada. Up close
telltale signs, brown stains

on the dash and upholstery, mute
predictable dolls with false eyelashes
and feigning sleep. Thus I evolve,
celebrant of the car-crash, and

contemplate the bruised colours
under lamplight. The wall
of reflecting hubcaps a constellation
of stars and minor planets; racks

of bumpers, grills, Crusaders' armour.
The Perfect Cold Warrior, ready
for anything: earthquake, Armageddon,
Social Credit. The world my gritty

oyster: insurance, commodities,
even journalism. My pulsing
proboscis picks up advance signals
of the Second Narrows Bridge collapse

hours before my father, with diving-suit
and acetylene torch, is recruited
to cut bodies from the Leggo
of twisted girders. Language, my stock

in trade, provides clues: *landslide,*
write-off, head-on, impending.
I align myself with Cassandra,
Suzuki, McNeil-Lehrer, I.F. Stone.

I think everyone loves calamity:
I come running with the latest bad news
only to be rebuked and set upon
outside the city gates.

2 *Palestine*

Everything we write
will be used against us
or against those we love.
These are the terms,
take them or leave them.
Poetry never stood a chance
of standing outside history.
— Adrienne Rich

Hanan

1

First night in the make-shift tent
I hardly slept. I couldn't stop
thinking of Daoud, unable
to protect himself from boots and

clubs as they dumped him, wrists
tied, in the back of the jeep. I twisted
for hours in that bruised borderland
of wakefulness, without relief.

Beds, of course, were destroyed
along with crockery. What was not ruined
by the force of the explosion was
scorched. I salvaged two aluminum pots

and a frying pan. One of the settlers
went through the rubble after the blast
smashing appliances and anything
of a personal nature. A sack of flour,

still intact, was dumped on the floor.
I could see his shoulders droop
and body arch slightly forward at the waist
the way men do when they urinate.

2

I awoke before the neighbours arrived
with the food and clothing they could spare,
but Hanan was gone and the single blanket
with which I'd covered her. I'd been

so upset over her brother and the house
I'd more or less ignored her, offering a kiss
but little else in the way of comfort.
How do you explain something like this

to a five-year-old? For a moment I panicked
thinking of the settler and his military
escort — a man who attributes
his rage and greed to God is capable

of anything — and the rabbi
who calls us West Bank Indians, favours
deportation, and wields his scriptures
like a scimitar. I ran crying

into the street. Nawal grabbed me
by the arm. Come, Mustafah
has found her. She's cold and a little
disoriented, but otherwise okay.

3

She'd appeared at Mustafah's door at sunrise
holding a red pencil and would eat
nothing until he gave her a piece of lined
paper, on which she reproduced letters

of the alphabet. I thanked them both
and took her back to the dozen or so tents
of the dispossessed families. She would not speak,
but sat quietly drawing circles

in the sand. Dr. el-Sarraj shook his head.
Time, he said, healing time. Take her
to visit Ali and Daoud in detention —
familiar faces. That night I watched her

slip from the tent when she thought
I was sleeping. I wanted to speak,
to run after her, but the doctor's words kept
sounding in my ears. I let her go,

put on my clothes, gathered up our blankets,
and stepped into the night air
among the shelters and scavenged objects.
You ask me where the anger is,

the outrage. Your committees thrive
on excess; so do my men. Isn't suffering
news enough? The phrase *refugees
in our own land* does cross my mind.

4

I recalled an incident on the coast near Jaffa
when we walked along the shore
barefoot, Daoud twirling his sister
so her feet scribed a transient

arc in the water. Scrolls of barbed wire
had been rolled aside to permit
bathing on a narrow strip of beach.
Three soldiers were laughing

and playing cards at a make-shift table
near the concession, so they did not notice
the Orthodox youth swagger past
with his uzi, sending a spray

of sand into the plate of olive oil
and hummus. He was no more than twelve,
Daoud's age at the time. Father and son,
seated on either side of me, tensed

to respond, but I placed a hand on Ali's
forearm and shook my head for Daoud's
benefit. The youth did not look back,
the soldiers continued with their game

of cards. Hanan, with a two-year-old's
self-absorpton, was amusing herself in the shade
of a towel, where she'd buried her plastic
doll to the neck, half-clothed, in the hot sand.

5

No urgency now. Curfew
had been lifted after the arrests
and demolitions. My pulse was racing
and my insides rumbled the way

they do when I make love to Ali.
He used to laugh and tease me
about being such an animal. Light
from the full moon reflected off the walls

and few remaining windows as I turned
the corner into our street. The beauty
of it made me want to weep. I eased myself
past the shattered door-frame and several

hanging timbers, catching the material
of my hem on a protruding nail. Some plaster
and rubble had been pushed aside
where the children's bedroom once stood

facing the garden, and I could just make
out the small figure curled up
in the dust, hands folded underneath
her head. I lay down too and took her in my arms.

Oranges & Oleander

I've grown accustomed to the scent of oranges,
oleander, the quiet exhilaration
of prayer.

Not always so. Before he arrived
in the village, I stood, artless, before the stunted
myths, sluggish, tormented, stripped
of all but my prodigal
desires.

Authorities paid me for information:
meetings, clandestine projects,
names mostly. I consumed large quantities
of wine, interviewed each animal
entering the ark.

Who was drinking at the well so early,
haloed in moonlight, a tangle
of stars still rampant
in the no longer indelible
night? He spoke, if he spoke at all,
in riddles.

Are we marsh-Arabs, he asked,
adrift in fertile estuaries, dependent
like bees on goodwill and pollen?
We perish from hunger,
while our poles sink three-feet deep

in the hidden source.

I broke my foot on the exposed
root. My squalid heart
gasped for breath, recalling its quarry-
stones, its shipwrecked
nuptials.

A lizard peered at me
from the stenographer's notebook
on my bedside table.
Rahed's body returned,
slit from neck to pelvic region.
Insult or organ harvest, the message
was clear.

Perfectly still except for the pulsing
green skin at his throat. Behind,
on the freshly polished wood surface,
the blue and white knitted kippie
of the Gush Emunim
might have been a mountain in Galilee.

Intricate perpendicular ribbing of the oleander.
Such beauty, such deadly leaves.
I drink only water
now.

Canada Park

*"The Israeli wars are a sort of continuation
of World War Two: the good guys
against the bad guys!"*
— Yehuda Amichai

Beneath the ancient branch
a bucket rests on its side, contents
of ripe fruit spilled on the close-cropped
grass. In the room my father's
typewriter taps the phrase
intoxicated dragonflies,
and pauses, intrigued but not quite
satisfied.

All we were thinking of
was sex. The girls, hair unbound
and disorderly, peered down
from the tallest tree. Slow
smiles, bodies ripe, angular, taut
like the strings of the *ud,*
daring us to pluck.

Together we watched the lamb's
birth, its raw blue cord
resplendent in straw as a magi's sash.
Sheep and the goats, my father
laughed. Shortly after
I was enrolled at a religious

school in Haifa. Plenty of time
to meditate on the nature
of good and evil
before I reached the age
of twelve.

My village had been replaced by a park,
imported trees. I stared a long time,
the typewriter in the backseat
unrelentingly critical
as ever. I searched for Christ
in the branches,
le mot juste,
and his anger filled me
as I looked at the crisp black lettering
of the sign.

In my father's house are many mansions . . .
Carpenter, stonemason, alien
tribe, the fingertip's
caress. Rhythm of passing
locomotive, boxcars.

Eyebrows, porticoes, stigmata,
the heart's Jihad.

Jordan

The rumbling bank, the impetuous river
bearing away my singing head.

Must it always end in exile,
the messenger's hand sent home,
packed in saffron?
Foreign voices
bending over to wash
garments, distant mountains
cloaked in an ochre haze.

"Station caravans, erect water towers,
dig defensive positions —
and proclaim it a settlement."

Can a city rise solely out of greed
in the desert? Pregnant women
stare from upper windows,
knives clenched in their teeth,
the bitter taste more than a chemical
reaction in the mouth.

It should have been a place of refuge
and refueling, relief from burning sun,
soil parched and arid, the nausea
of constant violence and fear,
stifling abstractions.

I went over, for a time, to the murderers,
forgetting God's name, agriculture, healing
waters. Masonry defected, flocks
assembled clandestinely
in the valley of the shadow, fields refused
the recently dead. Beware of words
that clamour to be spoken.

We are all Bedouins, itinerant
but territorial, our farthest boundaries
specific, even predictable.
Even. The first woman contained
in those letters. Locus,
oasis, garden we are all expelled from
but continue to tend.

Homeland

The place you were born in, where olive trees
planted by your grandfather's
grandfather are worn
smooth from the rubbing of goats.

Where you shacked-up
after your birthplace became hell, when
the fabled monsters stepped out of storybooks
into uniforms and positions
of power.

Real estate, dwellings you once lived in,
like the blue shingled bungalow
on 43rd Avenue with the gloomy
basement and sawdust burner,
or the flat above the laundromat
on Commercial Drive with urine stains
on the bathroom wallpaper.

Politics, its logistics and outer limits:
brinkmanship, lobbying, small settlements
or provinces thrown together
so Americans or Brits or someone else
wouldn't get a foothold, a
mandate. A maligne
or accidental residence for psychopaths
and other borderline
cases.

Race. The land God promised,
which you left when the going got rough
and Pharaoh made an offer
you could not refuse;
besides, that stunt with the Red Sea
was irresistible.

A state of mind. The continent
you pretended to discover, though
no one had reported it lost.

Call it the curse of geography,
of which some have too much, others
too little. Or history, *quelques arpents de neige*
ou desert, where your tribe
made the most news
or the most
money. *Not here, please,*
not here, where the only family you have
settles into the ecumenical ignominy
of a mass grave. You stand here
weeping, your apron pregnant
with medium-sized stones.
The womb, the womb!
An Eden you can't get back to
because your papers are not in order and exile
is a permanent condition.

Where does the soul
reside — marsh grasses, God's ear, or
that tender hollow at the base
of the lover's throat?

Green Line

For a while the salt taste of your shoulders
sustained me. I waited in line
before the single tap in the water-
main and did not envy
the freedom of migrating
birds. I recalled
wisps of grass,
your copper-coloured hair
smelling of jasmine,
but not the childhoods plundered
around us while the persecutors' offspring
were decked out in their finery
and sucked pomegranates.

Twenty-five years. Not even statistics
distracted me, compliant
in my rapture. Love is an enduring
occupation which matures, gives space
for other concerns, the green-
line separating youth
and age.

I read the history of my time
on tombstones. Epigrams,
not epics. Life pared
to the bone. A child fallen
in the street, struck

by a single bullet. Curses
rained down on his exploding
eardrums. An eye
for an insult; a bullet
for a stone, regardless
of origin.

Nights in Ansar II
we study, our nerves stringed instruments.
We take our medicine in modest
doses. The food is
scarce and bad. Even so,
I kiss your blessèd hands on this
our anniversary.

Rocks of Judea

"The Arabs are the rocks of Judea,
which must be removed from the path."
— Chaim Weizmann

I prowl the empty streets,
this stone a live coal in my hand,
divine tablet bearing the dates
'26, '48, '67, '82.

Profane lottery. And don't forget
854 and 878. I'm a human calculator,
malfunctioning, with spiralling accounts,
military orders closing schools.
Hours spent in line-ups
at the checkpoint, children restless, sick
from heat and carbon monoxide.
Indifference, the arbitrary
exercise of power.

I present the card, don't admit
to being other than I appear
under the lamination,
that there are two of me, a body
willing to be beaten
and dumped into an open
sewer, limbs tied in such awkward positions
that feet and hands are broken
for conferring behind backs,

58

bones so hard the soldiers had to
switch from wood to fibre-glass
truncheons.

                      Officially,
I don't exist. My name
appears on no list
of voters, my desires irrelevant
to the proper functioning
of the state. Yet someone
covets the space I inhabit,
submits a report
detailing my treason, engages
an architect's services.

Each morning weeds
push through my ribs, wind
whistles in my skull
cavity. On the cruel blackboard
of sky birds erase the features
of my face. What have I to lose
besides this stone, freighted
with humiliation,
desire?

I descend from the rooftop
no longer wrestling with God,
my conscience at ease,
seeking the immaculate one
who left a brother my age
at home in the midst

of computer games, a late snack
before bed-time. Young, full of promise,
but trained to smash faces,
rehearse obscenities.

I've come, by degrees, to love him,
ruddy, freckled, open
to experience, though not prepared
for the only perfect marriage
left to us, God's law
etched in stone.

It settles, jewel-like, in the fine
bones of his forehead,
beams at me.
                    Silent, forgiving,
cool now, and knowledgeable
as a third eye.

Twin sphinxes. We'll lie forever,
side by side, free at last
of politics, gender.

The Children's Envoy

We won't stay silent
under the earth, so much left unsaid,
undone. Our discord
cracks foundations;
our high-frequency messages
drive crazy your poets and domestic animals.

Above us the geography grows sour, acidic,
whole terrains turning to desert.

A fine dust settles in air-conditioners,
carburetors, rifle barrels,
until the engine of state grinds
to a halt. Lungs,
no longer able to resist,
give out. You view with revulsion
our swollen blue fingers
exposed to air in accusation
or greeting. Before you lost the gift
of prophecy, something
might have been done:
prayer, penitence, the usual.

Too late, you say, *get lost!*

Underground, our parliament
convenes. Lobbyists confer with Lazarus,
just as he is growing

lazy and acclimatized;
he accepts, reluctantly, the appointment
as ambassador, not, as
you'd expect, avenging angel.

Instead of a winding-sheet
he wears a garment resembling chain-mail,
a million black leathery hearts
shrunk to the size of peas,
varnished, threaded,
light as air.

He staggers along the white line
of the Jerusalem Road, face
a caucus of worms, arms
floundering, sea-legs
half restored. He can't escape
the sense of *déjà-vu.*

What you fear is not the eyes'
dark knowledge, cold
hands, corrupt stench invading
your nostrils, but the power
of diplomacy, the high sweet voice
raised in forgiveness
that will shatter everything
you know — glass partitions, protective
cages — and force you to
negotiate, begin
again.

Nablus, October

i

Too late for lemons and languor.
Beyond the walls idleness
skedaddles, eros
close behind.

An olive tree, blackened
by fire, glances over its shoulder
at the retreating azure
hills
       a tethered goat
ejaculates freely
on the confiscated dunams.

ii

At the town hall a man
in a wheelchair
recalls muscled legs
that carried him into the surrounding
hills, impact of blast, the car
cantilevered between two
entrances

and a painting of the prophet
invisible from crotch
down in the muddy waters

of the Jordan,
laughing while a disciple
douses him.

iii

Economies of scale.

Sabbath leaves
bale out, imperial summer's
taken to its heels

a beer can glints in sunlight
by the checkpost

What Does A House Want?

A house has no unreasonable expectations
of travel or imperialist ambitions;
a house wants to stay
where it is.

A house does not demonstrate
against partition or harbour
grievances;
                    a house is a safe
haven, anchorage, place
of rest.

Shut the door on excuses
— greed, political expediency.

A house remembers
its original inhabitants, ventures
comparisons:
                  the woman
tossing her hair
on a doorstep, the man
bent over his tools and patch
of garden.

What does a house want?

Laughter, sounds
of love-making, to strengthen
the walls;
                    a house
wants people, a permit
to persevere.

A house has no stones
to spare; no house has ever been convicted
of a felony, unless privacy
be considered a crime in the new
dispensation.

What does a house want?

Firm joints, things on the level, water
rising in pipes.

Put out the eyes, forbid
the drama of exits,
entrances.   Somewhere
in the rubble a mechanism
leaks time,
                    no place
familiar for a fly
to land
on

3 Norwegian Rabbit
(The Trotsky Poems)

. . . a book should be the axe for the frozen sea within us.

— Franz Kafka

Prologue

Leon Trotsky's final days were spent in Coyoacan,
a suburb of Mexico City, where he and his wife
and entourage were guests at the infamous 'Blue
House' of Frida Kahlo and Diego Rivera. After
an extended period, the Trotskys moved a few
blocks away to 45 Calle Viena, where he carried
on his writing and political activities against a
background of hostility from the pro-Stalin
Mexican Communist Party. An attempt, led by
Rivera's rival muralist David Siqueiros, was made
on Trotsky's life, during which his American
bodyguard Robert Sheldon Harte mysteriously
disappeared and was later found murdered.
Having been deported from Russia, Turkey,
France, and Norway, Trotsky was grateful for
his Mexican haven, despite its obvious dangers,
and spent his spare time collecting rare cacti,
raising chickens and rabbits, and contemplating
the fate of the revolution in a world locked in
mortal combat. So it was on that fateful morning
in August 1940, when he rose early to prepare
himself for work on the Lenin biography, several
articles and letters to editors, and an appointment
he had agreed to reluctantly . . .

1

When the Norwegians kicked us out
and we sailed to Mexico in the tanker *Ruth*,
we had icebergs on the starboard side;
on port, the Gulf Stream. I could taste
the continent as we passed
Newfoundland and New England.

Returning from my previous exile the ship
stopped in Halifax, where the circumspect Canadians
wouldn't allow me ashore;
then they arrested the whole family
and held us in detention.
Nothing new in that.

I rise early to feed my rabbits and chickens
in their cages and observe my cacti in the clear light
and cool air of the morning.

Most days I stay bent over my labours
like a monk. Newspapers, essays
commissioned by friends
of Dewey, Breton, and Niebhur,
and the biography of Lenin.
A prisoner of my house,
my convictions.

Then the smells draw me out to Veracruz
or Pátzcuaro. Hills, tender landscapes,
and the blinding light of the Gulf. Picnics,
fishing, always more plants.

When we return from one of these outings
Natalia Sedova begins to tease me. Leon Davidovitch,
she laughs, nature has restored you yet again.
You smile, your eyes are blue and clear
as the sky. I think, at heart,
you're a simple peasant.

Hot and cold, the way winds blow
from the Left. The Spanish phrase for lemming
is *conejo de noruega.*

Norwegian rabbit.

2

Icicles in St. Petersberg, my school friend
Ivan carefully breaking off
the largest and doing his cavalry
charge across the square.

This journey to warmth,
the only snow visible at the rim
of Popo.
                    Gathering cactus
along the dirt roads. How it survives,
hoarding essentials deep inside,
defended by sharp needles,
words that pierce.

This tiny country, rooted
in history: *los indios,*
artists so vibrant and passionate —
those who do not embrace you
and offer refuge rise up
to kill you. Was it loyalty to the Party
or my friendship with Frida
and Diego that inspired Siqueiros
to attack the residence at Calle Viena?
A thing about walls. Later,
they found Robert Sheldon Harte,
my American bodyguard, dead
in the Desert of the Lions.

By the time we finish
reinforcements, reducing the size
of windows and bricking-in
the balcony, my beloved casa
resembles a bunker.

3

Outside, I hear the clucking of my chickens;
in here, the click of the dictating-machine
we've nicknamed "Little Joseph."

It's not easy to spread in public Stalin's dirty linen,
to admit the revolution was betrayed and sullied
by a bully and psychopath. I told the Dewey
Commision the show trials were a juridical play,
the roles prepared in advance.

My demand for "permanent revolution" advocates
pruning and renewal to keep the bureaucracy
from promoting privilege.

I've tried to make the point more than once
that Stalin had nothing to do with constructing
the Soviet machine of state; he simply
used it for his own ends.
In his hands the apparatus grew rigid,
monstrous. I described him
at the time of the October Revolution
as "a grey spot which would sometimes give out
a dim and inconsequential light."

Husbandry is not his strongest suit.

4

The woman writing for *The Tribune* asked me
how it felt to be a hero of the revolution.

She was on assignment in Mexico City
and had large feet, protruding
from the kind of hand-made
sandals sold in the Zócalo. The nail
of each big toe was square as a window.

I was shocked. First, by the Americanness
of the query, the blatant interest
in individualist mythology. Second,
by her audacity in thinking I'd actually
answer such a question. I laughed. I could
as easily have chosen anger. Writing
for the Left, she must have expected me
to say the people are the real heroes
of the revolution, that leaders
are mere tentacles grown, or evolved,
to serve the interests of the people.

Instead, I said I felt like Dr. Frankenstein,
who had created a monster that was
out of control. Her turn to pretend
shock at my deviation from the Party line.

She closed her green spiral notebook
and leaned forward. The severity
with which her hair was pulled back
gave her an Asian aspect

and the thickness of the lenses
made her brown eyes even larger
in their narrow envelopes.

You've got it all wrong. The monster was
an innocent who never understood
the world's response to him. In the end,
he carried the body of his beloved creator,
who deserted and tried to kill him,
to rest among the ice-floes. You

should be so lucky. I suspect
the truth lies elsewhere and you believe
history made *you*, the old
materialist scapegoat. She pulled
one large, unbound, American
foot into her lap and rubbed
the squared nail with her thumb.

5

I should have spent time with my children,
two daughters who waved to me from the crowds
as I was passed overhead towards the exit
of the Modern Circus in Petrograd. So much
pride and pain in their troubled faces:
orphans of ideology.

When I wasn't kept up half the night
addressing the assembled crowds in that building,
workers, castoffs, infants at their mother's breasts,
children on shoulders, I was being wakened at five
and taken by tug to talk to the navy boys
at Krondstadt.

The electric tension of that impassioned human throng,
to quote myself. I chucked my prepared notes
on the floor and was taken over by some extra sense,
an unconscious reserve of empathy that told me
what they needed to hear, the whole crowd
hanging on like that, *infants sucking with their dry lips
the nipples of revolution.*

My opponents picked up the refrain soon enough,
shouting down my speeches or ideas
by saying: " This ain't your Modern Circus."

6

A number of yellow-jackets reconnoitering
the new brickwork. If they're not spying for the GPU
or Siqueiros, they might be seeking refuge
in new ideas. Syvlia's beau Frank Jacson
arrives shortly to show me the second draft
of a confused and indifferent article
about divisons among French Trotskyites.
He should stick to the business
of exports and bring Sylvia instead,
who is helpful and without pretentions.

Avispa, the Spanish for wasp, also means
"sly-sort," "wily-bird," or in common Mexican usage,
"thief." Waspish, for "quick-tempered",
de prontos enojos. Avispero:
wasp's nest, or medical
figure of speech for the inflammation
known as a carbuncle. *Con talle de avispa*:
wasp-waisted. *The Dictionary of American Slang*
sent to me from Chicago has twenty-five expressions
to describe an attractive girl.

Yellow-jackets, yellow journalism. I spend
too much time learning languages, acquiring the tools
of wisdom but not wisdom itself. And what about
the blue-jackets at Krondstadt, so supportive
at first, asking my advice in prison
from their cruiser?

7

Frida and Diego made plans to take me
to the coast, staying in the small village
of Barra de Navidad, where one of his patrons
or hangers-on had provided a beach-house
with three rooms and a sprawling veranda
fully screened. They promised a surprise guest,
but would not divulge his name.

Diego poured tequila while we talked art,
politics, stroganoff. Shadows
played across their glistening faces
with every flicker of the coal-oil wick.
Frida tamped and lit a pipe. Each time
she lifted her thumb from the bowl
it made a sound
like the popping of a small cork.
Several large, grey moths, having reconnoitered
the screened porch, fastened themselves
to the wire gauze. More of my gypsy
relatives, our guest said. Spies,
Diego offered. Frida spat,
expelling a strand of tobacco.
A screen test, she replied, *nada mas.*
When I asked him about working
with Lang on *The Third Man,* he smiled.
Wrong man, he said, though I've seen enough
to make my eyes bug-out like that. Diego's
paintings, for example, could transform an eagle
into a hyper-thyroid case.

Edward G. Robinson had driven from Hollywood
in his capacity as art collector. This village,
he confided to the assembled spirits
of evening, is too ramshackle
to be called quaint, but it takes its living
from the sea, not to mention evolutionary relics
like ourselves, who gather on the very seam
of our liberation, or expulsion,
from the source. The question, my dear friends,
is this: Do we come to mourn
or to celebrate?

At mid-morning he walked with me,
pantlegs rolled up, taking refuge
in wet sand. His footprints
were half the size of mine. We watched
the waves erase them equally.
Ah, democracy! he sighed.
When I spoke of the positive response
my articles received in his country,
Edward G. tossed a flat stone he'd picked up
near the house. It bounced several times
across the water and disappeared
into the curl of a wave. Paint or tar,
he said, Americans don't discriminate;
they use the same brush for both. Sooner or later
they'll cut our legs off, at the knees.

When I failed, at first, to catch his meaning,
he spun in my direction, took a deep breath
and held it until his cheeks and eyes
bulged. Then he rubbed his hands unctuously,
and in the familiar nasal accent
of Peter Lorre, whispered:

"Señor Trotsky, it pains me to say this,
but you shpick Yiddish mit a Brooklyn accent."

8

Sometimes I see the face of my father.
Lev Bronstein, he says. Was your given name
not good enough, or are you just ashamed
of being a Jew? My Jewish origins
were not an issue as long as I was not in the public
eye. Anti-Semitisim raised its head
with that of anti-Trostkyism.

My Last Will and Testament is largely a tribute
to Natalia Ivanovna Sedova who, as the saying goes,
stood by me in all manner of troubles.
In fact, she stood *on* me, when necessary,
so I wouldn't run off half-cocked.
She admired my jokes more than my politics
and the one line of mine she took
for her motto was "Myself,
I am not a Trostkyite." Women
in the revolution; another chapter
still to be written. I admired Emma Goldman
in principle — fiery, dynamic — but I never enjoyed
her breathless pontificating, which smacks of rhetoric,
however sincere. Disillusioned with Soviet politics
she retreated to Canada. Enough said.

I prefer the working-class intelligence
of *The Autobiography of Mother Jones*,
a book I could see myself translating.
Organizing coal-miners in Philadelphia

and West Virginia and still active
at ninety-three, when she joined
the Farm-Labour Party. Her reluctance
to dwell on adversities sustains me
all these years after Zinaida's suicide in Berlin,
the loss of my manuscripts in the fire
that destroyed our house in Prinkipo,
the murder of Lyova in Paris,
not to mention Stalin, the rise of Facism,
etcetera, etcetera, just as it sustained me
in 1935 on the lawn at Honefoss
outside Oslo, as I recuperated from the factions
and in-fighting that plagued our days
in France. The answer, father, is no:

I'm not ashamed to be a Jew, but sometimes
I'm ashamed to be a man.

9

When I was a boy, Kasimir Antonovich sold me
a sack of pigeons. I crawled through his filthy attic
in the dark to catch them unawares. Ivan Vasilyevich
helped grab them but all hell broke loose
after they uncovered the lantern. There were cobwebs
in my eyes and the smell of mouse droppings
filled my nostrils. And all to no avail — except,
of course, as education — since, after we'd built
our own loft and equipped it for breeders,
they all flew back to their former residence.

I'll spare you the obvious political
analogies. What if the proleteriat
cannot rule, what if they fail to achieve
revolutionary consciousness? Lenin
might have found a way. At least his dialectic
was expansive. Take Comrade Martov — he could
make a watch that would tell time accurately,
but Lenin knew the laws of the earth's motion
around its axis. I lie awake at night thinking
of my beloved Lyova, allergic to dust
and certain insect bites, who was found wandering
in the hospital corridors after his operation in Paris,
poisoned, delirious. He wanted nothing
to do with Mexico or chickens.

Kasimir Antonovich married a beautiful woman
but died a year later, when a bull gored him.
I imagine him thrusting the sack of pigeons
in my face and saying: Pay attention, Lev Davidovich,
everything comes home to roost.

9

I've become, by default, a specialist
in chicken psychology. Behold
my disciples, my devoted audience!

Zinoviev here, with the clipped wings
and tilted head, was described as "panic itself"
during the seige of Petrograd. He spends
his time in blissful spasms or prostrate
on the couch, in response to reports
from the front. He'll survive, of course,
and thrive on bueaucracy. Next to him,
comb bristling, is General Krasnov,
elegant but unreliable with his traitorous
alliances. Ladies, beware! He fancies
Kseshinskaya, our fancy dancer, once
a favourite of the Czar, who hangs out
with the rabbits, eating their greens
and dreaming of fur coats. Larissa,
like her namesake, flashes across the garden,
a meteor, blinding mere mortals.
She was prominent in the Fifth Army,
in intelligence, then in writing brilliant sketches
about the civil war. Larissa's career
will burn brightly, but not long.

I leave till last Rosa Luxemburg, whom I admired
always, from a distance. Sickly but noble,
with eyes that radiate intelligence. Rosa
is subtle and merciless in her assessment
of ideas and strategies. I find myself

in this whirlpool by accident, she says;
I should have been tending geese
in the fields. Rosa, blessed Rosa,
you take comfort only among cacti.

And the egg itself? An imperfect sphere
of possibility. Obdurate, said
to be unbreakable if pressure is applied
equally at all points.

11

In the company of Jean Van Heijenoort
we took a train from Paris to Antwerp,
then sailed to Oslo. We can't seem to escape
our French connections, Van said, pointing out
the name *Paris* on the ship's bulkhead.
Our new hosts may view this ship
as a Trojan Horse, I replied.

I was thinking of the series of flip-flops
of the Norwegian Labour Government, which
granted a visa, cancelled, then reinstated it for a six-
month period. Our reception would be anything
but enthusiastic. Apart from Konrad Knudsen,
who gave us the use of his house, and a few others,
the Norwegians were asleep. War, the Revolution,
and the upheavals of fascism, had passed them by
without a trace. Your future, I teased Konrad,
consists only of hot and cold showers. Now
more than weather holds them in thrall.

By sea we travelled more or less
incognito, thanks to Turkish
émigré passports and the extreme barbering
I submitted to in Grenoble.
The garrulous Figaro refused, at first, to cut
my hair short as he thought it looked
distinguished, professorial; then he began to suspect
I was trying to disguise my identity and
went on about giving me a Chaplin moustache.

We heard of the expulsion of pliant Enukidze,
the murder of Antipov, while news of the trials
heated up in the press along with the rumour
that I had tried illegally to enter Norway
on a previous occasion. After a short reprieve,
I collapsed again from nervous exhaustion, broken,
unable to eat, read, or think. *Rien.*

12

Passionate? Yes, but also lame and certainly
not wasp-waisted. By the time we met
Frida was spending whole days in a wheelchair
or in hot baths for relief. It's fair to say
I was taken with her wit, crude
humour, and almost primitive intelligence.

We were installed in the Blue House
in Coyoacan and spent too long in the role
of honoured guests for anyone to tolerate.
My work went on, regardless. In arguments
she often took my side, infuriating Diego,
especially after his periodic absences.
The intimacy she insinuated was meant
to make him jealous. I wasn't immune
to her game: flattering an old man with headaches
and high blood-pressure. Predictably,
I couldn't concentrate on writing
when she sat in the same room with a book.

The blow-up came when I tried to explain
the "neither war nor peace" strategy
which had guided our negotiations
with the Kaiser's minions in Brest-Litovsk.
Diego was drinking heavily and Frida,
as conspicuously as possible, placed the bottle
of tequila just beyond his reach. Natalia Sedova
had abandoned diplomacy for bed,

but the door to our room was slightly ajar,
so I knew she was not sleeping. Diego
could not be convinced that the stalling tactics
had succeeded and kept pointing out
the harsher terms of the eventual peace agreement.
He was a good Communist, but pressure
from the Stalinist trade unions to sever connections
with me was building. It's perfectly obvious,
Frida announced, turning her chair dismissively
in my direction. He grabbed her cane
and pulled the tequila towards him with the crook,
drinking straight from the bottle. Frida's
smile froze him in that position for several seconds
before the bottle shattered on the table edge.

Several chairs were overturned as he made his way
through the house to the street, cursing.
As I realized later, he was sober enough
to make a linguistic distinction between the verbs
stall and *delay*. Peace was delayed by fog,
but Trotsky, he said, has stalled in this house
for two years. In the silence that followed,
I could hear the click of Natalia Sedova's door.

13

We'd made some sort of peace with the Americans,
whose country was born in revolution
and forged in civil war. But England was another
matter altogether. After driving Yudenich
from the gates of Petrograd back across
the Finnish border, with his English backing,
superior forces and advanced technology,
anti-English feeling was so intense I felt a need
to educate my troops and wrote the following memo:

> *Besides the England of profits, of violence, bribery,*
> *and bloodthirstiness, there is the England*
> *of labour, of spiritual power, of high ideals*
> *of international solidarity. It is the base and*
> *dishonest England of stock-exchange manipulators*
> *that is fighting us. The England of labour*
> *and the people is with us.*

As War Commissar I inherited
an impossible situation. We had to substitute
improvisation for a system that did not
exist. Though I erred on the side of pedantry,
my observations were basically sound.
Most of them. When one of our automobiles,
mounted with machine-guns, became stuck in mid-
stream, I cursed its low-slung engine. Puvi,
my Estonian driver, lifted his cap and said:
"I beg to state that the engineers never foresaw
we should have to sail on water."

A brick, as the English say. If only
I could see Puvi again, and my train crew,
none of whom would question my integrity
or go on about Krondstadt.

14

Condemned, by bad health, to the reading of novels.

If Stalin doesn't kill me first, popular culture
will do the trick. No grace, no artistry,
not even an idea to burn. Confirms my view
of the English bourgeoisie as cultivated savages,
who gape at processions of royalty
and enjoy reading Edgar Wallace's novels.

I was equally disgusted by the sorcery of Lourdes,
trafficking in trinkets and miracles to scare and uplift
the little people. And the papal blessing transmitted
by radio waves. The chief Roman druid
disgracing a proud technology. How ironic
that my nickname in coded letters from Lyova
was "Crux." Trotsky, the cross contemporary history
refuses to bear; yet organ-destroying microbes
may cross the finish-line first.

Old age is the most unexpected thing
that happens to a man.

15

Whose is this disembodied voice
talking about translation? I'll soon be
translated bodily, but not to heaven.
A junkyard for dead materialists,
rather, where the parts can be recycled.

Lenin coined that phrase, I believe.
I first heard him use it in Petrograd,
in relation to the terrible waste
of talent in purges. Decades of industrial
and professional know-how sacrificed
for the fleeting satisfactions of revenge.
He made a strong case for integrating
the old guard, believing political
re-education would bring them round
to our way of thinking. No alternative,
really, with war on our doorstep
and chaos looming. Some of the officers
came on board to save their skins.
The professional soldiers amongst them
recognized a job to be done and had
no trouble switching allegiance.
Their fifedoms were *le petit pays*
of the cruiser or battalion;
their pride, the well-oiled machine
doing its job. In extreme heat
the quality of reproduction deteriorates
and my new toy threatens to malfunction
— even disembodied voices

can be erased or rendered unrecognizable.

Still, I prefer to think aloud in private;
otherwise, I get distracted trying
to imagine what impact my words
might be having on the stenographer.
I keep wanting to interject: Does that make
any sense? Have I made myself
perfectly clear? Consider this my hymn
in praise of the dictaphone, a tribute
to Little Joseph's mechanical ear
and unfailing memory. Liberating,
impersonal as a crowd.

16

Truly intellectual creation is incompatible with lies,
hypocrisy, and the spirit of conformity.
Yes, there's no more than a passing reference
to the Krondstadt uprising in *My Life*. The sailors
were conned by agitators and Old Guard officers
we hadn't properly educated. They proclaimed
a "new revolution" and sent their demands
by telegraph to Moscow and Petrograd.

After some hesitation, I ordered the Red Army
to attack across the ice. Food was scarce,
the country was in the grip
of unseasonable cold. It's said a man
sees his own death years or decades
in advance of the event. As a child I believed
I'd be found frozen in a snowbank
like the blonde heifer, its legs
tucked underneath in a vain effort
to conserve heat. Exile to warmth
seemed a reprieve. Cognition emanates
from the intersection of nature
and consciousness. The latter serves
as a movie-camera extracting moments
from uninterrupted nature and presenting them to us
interrupted, in a manner that exploits the eye's
imperfection. I'm echoing Vertov
and the others. Film, everything silent
except the theorists. The ice at Krondstadt
was red with blood that wouldn't
wash away until spring.

17

The old plugs that worked our farm
in the Ukraine would look like drawings
of shaggy prehistoric beasts by the end
of the first month of winter. Politicians, too,
hair-up against the abrasions of public life,
though they are not nearly so useful as draft horses
and seldom pull their weight or learn to forage
in deep snow. Stalin grew a thick skin
and surrounded himself with a protective coating
of flunkies and psychophants. Bukharin, a
perfectionist, a detail man, could not tolerate
uncertainty or compromise; he was a liability,
or worse, during the seige of Petrograd.

The assassin has no difficulty locating the weak spot,
the Achilles heel, in these soon-to-be-extinct
creatures. Myself am blind to the failings
of those who love words, ideas. A book
or essay is sufficient passport.

18

Where is Frank Jacson? He looked ill
during his last visit, dehydrated and a little green
around the gills. He carried an old overcoat
on his arm and deposited himself
on the edge of the desk while I tried to make sense
of his convoluted prose. I did not object
to this or the unremoved hat, lest I encourage him
to stay, interrupting further the stout attack
on pacificism I was pouring in the metal ear
of Little Joseph. He took himself off
with the article, my few suggestions,
and the offer of a second visit.

France has capitulated. England, finally,
has something worse to endure than the novels
of Edgar Wallace, as aerial bombardment
continues. I remember André saying,
while we talked with Diego in the garden
of the Blue House, "Surrealism will not prevent war,
but it will make an endurable peace."
From that discussion, and our collective forays
against socialist realism, I articulated my view
that art can be the revolution's great ally only insofar
as it remains true to itself.

I wish he were still here — Breton, that is.

19

I was criticized for not fraternizing,
not putting in appearances at the ballet
or giving lavish parties for my friends
and associates. Socializing — is this
what it means to be a socialist?

Shrewd as I am said to be in terms
of theory, I lack a capacity
for intrigue. Ferocious in defense
of revolution, to quote Lenin,
yet I formed no alliances
to protect me against calumny,
careerists. Society bores me,
though individuals may be as curious
and engaging as books. Take
Cardenas, for example. No, not
el presidente who granted me asylum.
I don't move in those circles
anymore. Frida's gardener, who'd
lost a leg fighting for Zapata
near Veracruz, confessed quite openly
his faith in vegetables. Fallen
in one of the hacienda's cultivated
fields, he'd made a tourniquet
from grape vines, then stuffed himself
with tomatoes and carrots before
passing out. *I've devoted my life
to vegetables, not politics.* Brown face
a nest of furrows, yet the smile

unmistakable beneath his hat brim.
Squinting into sunlight and using
the shovel-handle for balance
as he rolls another cigarette.

Sometimes I listen to my own voice
on the wax recording surface
and have to laugh. I have no talent
for small-talk, though I can hold forth
for hours on points of doctrine,
or certain species of plant.

Don't get me started on cacti.

Cardenas' artificial leg, scrubbed
and drying by the adobe wall,
rises from its detachable
foot like an exclamation mark.

He takes the drink I offer,
raises an arm in mock salute:

¡Viva Patata!

20

Sieva, my beloved granchild, spends too much time
in this prison, consulting with ancients
who go about their dubious affairs
under the threat of death.

He loves the rabbits as much as I do
and will not go to bed without reading to them
in German from the book of fairy tales,
his last gift from Zinaida. He'll soon
be the only Bronstein left. Safer, perhaps,
than bearing the name of Volkow,
another of Stalin's million expendable
fathers. He knows the three guards
on the street by name and asks
Moreño for leftover greens from his wife's
mother's restaurant. The attack troubled him
less than Robert's disappearance
and subsequent death.

I remarked last week how light from the gooseneck
lamp gathers about his eybrows, knitted
in concentration. Natalia says
he "positively shines with intelligence"
and insists her assessment is entirely devoid
of the subjectivity of grandmothers.

He studies the map of Mexico in my office
and already knows the regions and their capitals,
not to mention their chief agricultural
products. He learns more of rabbits
than of Bolsheviks in this establishment.

21

Three weeks later, with the spring thaw,
Krondstadt would have become impregnable,
haven for every reactionary and malcontent.

So much for my sailor boys, once the pride and glory
of the revolution, who helped eliminate Kerensky
and his lackies. Their horticultural commune,
housing committees, and talk about returning power
to the local Soviets didn't fool me. Fourteen
clandestine issues of *Izvestia.* I read every one
and watched the rhetoric grow more inflammatory
by the day. Kotlin was our only sure defence
against attack from the Gulf of Finland,
an island fortress where they were free
to conduct monster rallies in Anchor Square
and crank out counter-revolutionary propaganda
without interference. I dropped a few bombs
in their midst and warned them they'd be shot
like partridges. They refused to turn over Skurikhin
from on board the battleship *Petropavlovsk,*
attacking me verbally as a dictator, an evil genius,
and comparing me with Maliuta Skouratoff,
the scourge of Ivan the Terrible, and the Tzarist
General Trepoff, who advised his troops
not to economize on bullets. I followed
their advice. I took nothing personally. Instead,
I took the measure of yoeman Petrichenko,
who could use metaphor to persuade;
he, not Sklovsky, was spokesman and leader
of the revolt. No ordinary seaman,

he spoke of seizing the rudder from the Communists
and sailing the re-fit Soviet vessel to Petrograd,
then to all of Russia. I had to act, being one
of the warned-against shoals. They were no fools,
even if they misspelled Yudenich. "Listen, Trotsky,"
he wrote, "as long as you succeed in escaping
judgment, you can shoot innocent
persons in batches. But you cannot shoot the truth."

Being called a butcher in wartime is no great insult
— no room there for weakness or hesitation —
but to be accused by a puffed-up traitorous rating
of destroying truth. If they wanted General Trepoff,
that's what they'd get. No bullets spared.

22

I should have dismissed Jacson
for his impertinence, never mind the vacuity
and wrong-headedness of his article.
Forced, in my exile, to suffer fools and play
the teacher. No reminders of my iron fist
except an alarm button and revolver
mired in this blizzard of correspondence.

The heavy guns from Krasnia Gorka
were enough to soften them up, while troops
and cavalry moved under cover of fog
across the ice. The first assault in white
camouflaged uniforms had been repulsed
and decimated by machine-gun fire;

those who returned were useless, dragging
frozen, blood-encrusted comrades,
half-crazy in their ragged ghostly shrouds.

I appointed Dybenko Commissar of Krondstadt
and gave him the task of cleaning up
the city. Those partridges that survived the massacre
of March 17 were rounded up and shot,
not one but could have lived as simply
and as well as these chickens
if they'd brought their needs to our attention
without challenging authority.

23

Why did Robert open my door to Siqueiros
and his gang and later appear
to be getting into the car of his own volition?
I can't believe he was a piece of Stalinist shit.

What's happening to my mind, my style?
I shift with such ease to a street-fighter's idiom
that would melt the wax cylinders of Little Joseph.
Sylvia tells me Jacson carries a forged
Canadian passport to avoid conscription
in Belgium. We'll see how he avoids
intellectual frostbite.

Comrades Kuzmin and Kalinin addressed the delegates
of the Provisional Revolutionary Committee
in Anchor Square in Krondstadt on March 1,
with sixteen thousand sailors, soldiers, and workers
in attendance. They attacked the resolutions,
but their speeches had no effect. Incompetents.
I could have brought the doubters round, appealing
to old loyalties, drawing the leadership into our circle,
at least temporarily. Prisons were anathema
to those free spirits; ideas circulated
without persecution. How similar our positions
seem now, as I assume the siege mentality,
sending my paper planes across fogbound ice,
against the thunderous fusilades from Lissy Noss.

I said to Natalia only this morning:
"What's this, we've slept another night
without being killed and you're not happy?"

24

The cactus evolved spines to keep from being
devoured and enable it
to collect moisture from arid
and semi-arid environments. This, in turn,
is carried by grooves to the roots of the plant.
Even then, various species are nearing extinction
as a result of climatic changes and damage
brought on by human encroachment.

I hear voices in the garden. Frank Jacson
has arrived and is making small talk
with the guards. It's not the least bit cold,
but he's wearing a hat and still carrying
that shabby gaberdine overcoat.

Lemmings and lovers. How quickly
salesmen learn to break the ice.

I see why Sylvia is smitten
by his attentions. He can't write
or keep two ideas in the air at the same time,
yet he's attentive as a domestic animal.

Even the chickens are aflutter.

Notes

It is impossible to know, with any degree of certainty, the extent to which events at Krondstadt figured in Trotsky's subsequent conscious and subconscious life. I have used this incident in the history of the Russian revolution, where I might have used the suppression of the Makhnovist Movement in the Ukraine, because the rebellion at Krondstadt took place in a single dramatic locale and in a manageably brief period of time.

To shape this interior monologue, I have made use of the following books, quoting Trotsky's own words where useful or unavoidable: *My Life* by Leon Trotsky, *Trotsky's Notebooks: 1933-1935, Trotsky's Diary in Exile: 1935, The Unknown Revolution: 1917-1921* by V. M. Eikhenbaum (*nom de plume,* Voline), and two short Mexican publications: *Leon Trotsky: Su Asilo En Mexico* and *Museo Casa De Leon Trotsky: Memoria de su restauración.*